swinging jazz

contents

ISBN 978-1-4234-6020-6

HAL•LEONARD®

7777 W. BLUEMOUND RD. P.O. BOX 13819 MILWAUKEE, WI 53213

T0057701

Visit Hal Leonard Online at
www.halleonard.com

AIN'T THAT A KICK IN THE HEAD

Words by SAMMY CAHN
Music by JAMES VAN HEUSEN

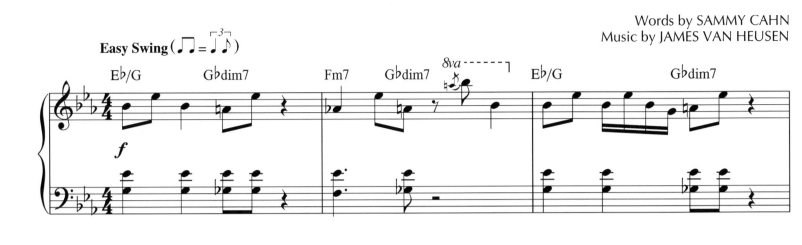

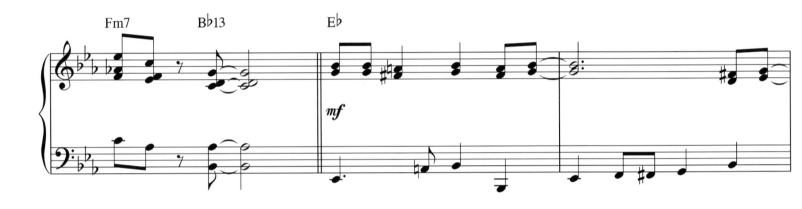

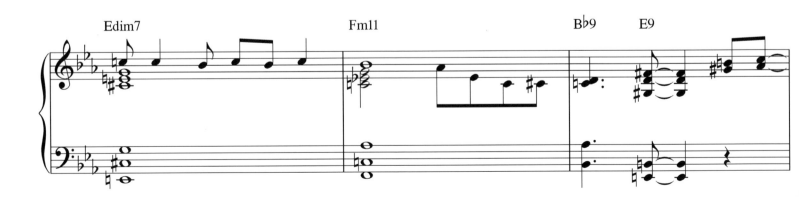

BALLIN' THE JACK

Words by JIM BURRIS
Music by CHRIS SMITH

ALL OF ME

Words and Music by SEYMOUR SIMONS
and GERALD MARKS

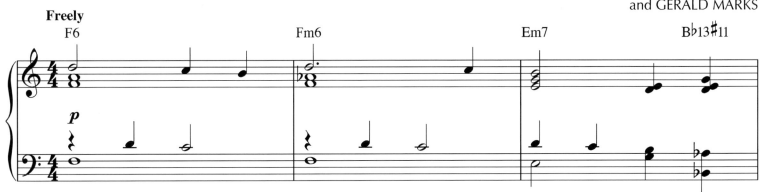

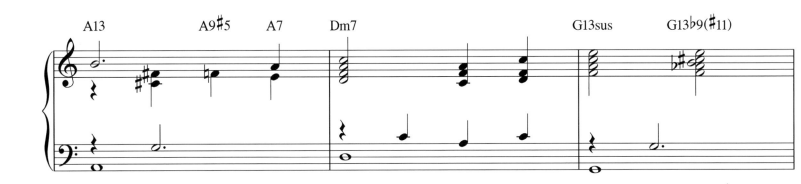

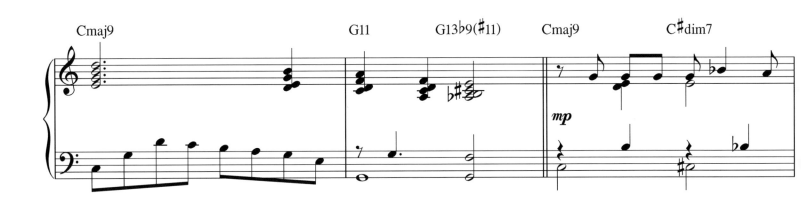

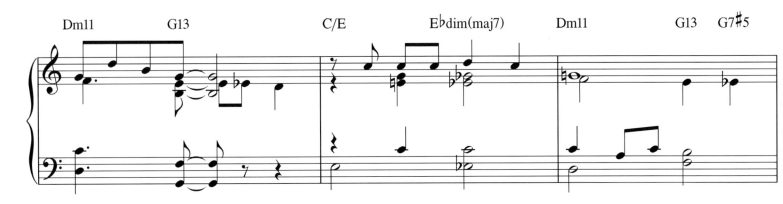

BEYOND THE SEA

By ALBERT LASRY
and CHARLES TRENET
English Lyrics by JACK LAWRENCE

THE HUCKLEBUCK

By ANDY GIBSON

16

BLUESETTE

Words by NORMAN GIMBEL
Music by JEAN THIELEMANS

Moderately, lightheartedly (♩♩ = ♩♩)

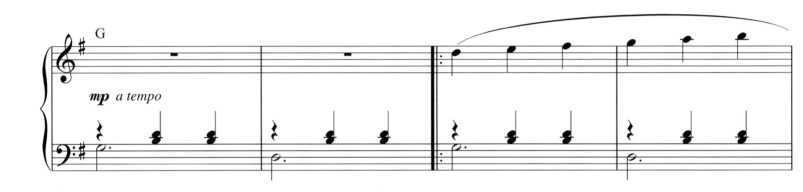

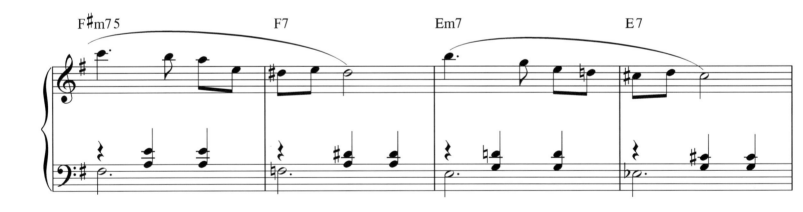

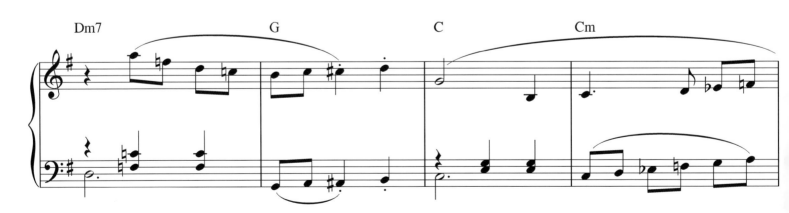

COME FLY WITH ME

Words by SAMMY CAHN
Music by JAMES VAN HEUSEN

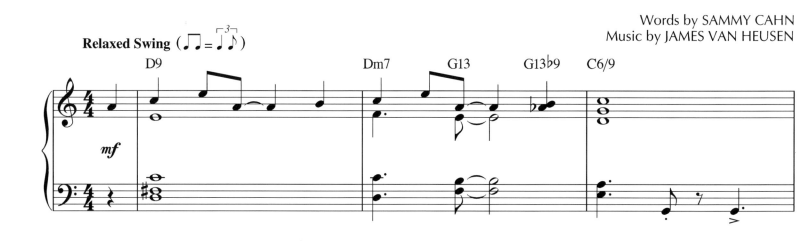

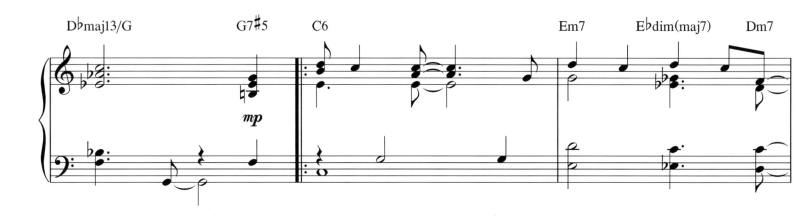

'DEED I DO

Words and Music by WALTER HIRSCH
and FRED ROSE

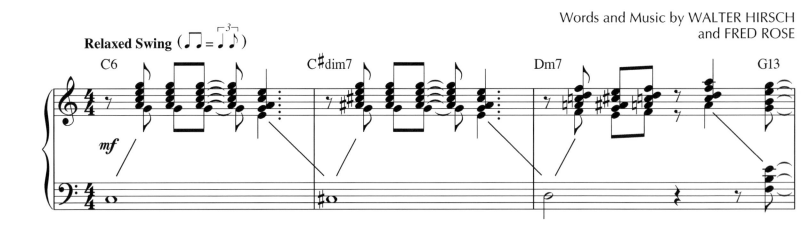

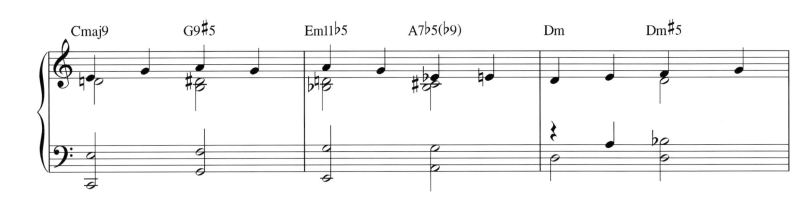

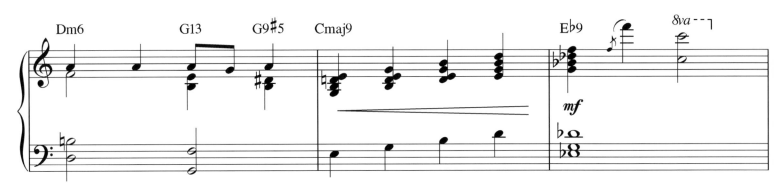

THE FRIM FRAM SAUCE

Words and Music by JOE RICARDEL
and REDD EVANS

GEE BABY, AIN'T I GOOD TO YOU

Words by DON REDMAN
and ANDY RAZAF
Music by DON REDMAN

Slow Blues

GIRL TALK
from the Paramount Picture HARLOW

By NEAL HEFTI

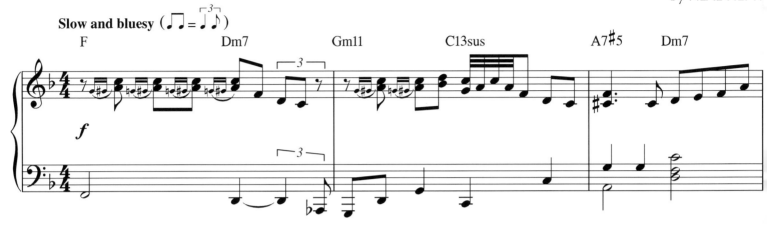

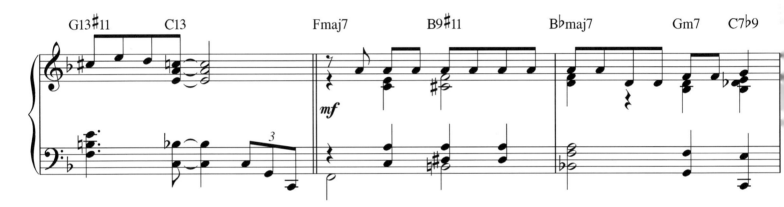

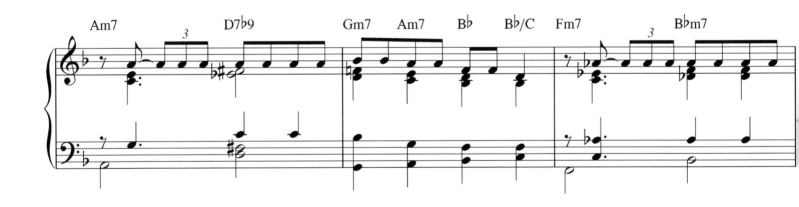

GRAVY WALTZ

Lyrics by STEVE ALLEN
Music by RAY BROWN

*First chorus based on one by Oscar Peterson.

IT'S ONLY A PAPER MOON

Lyric by BILLY ROSE and E.Y. "YIP" HARBURG
Music by HAROLD ARLEN

JUST IN TIME

from BELLS ARE RINGING

Words by BETTY COMDEN
and ADOLPH GREEN
Music by JULE STYNE

Moderate Swing

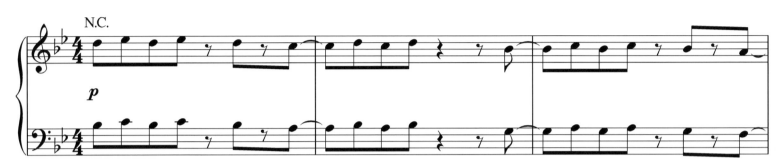

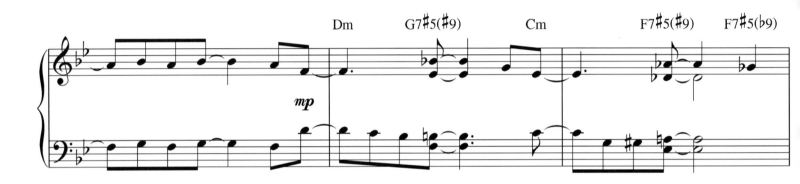

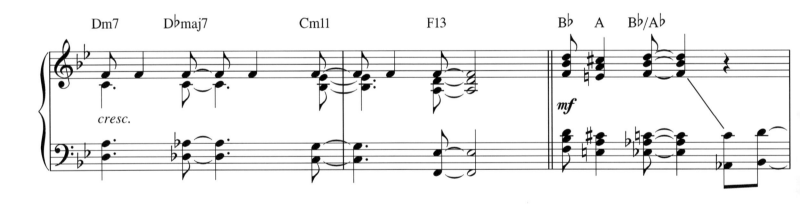

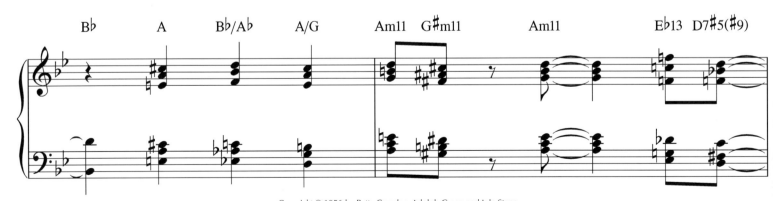

LIKE YOUNG

Words and Music by PAUL WEBSTER
and ANDRÉ PREVIN

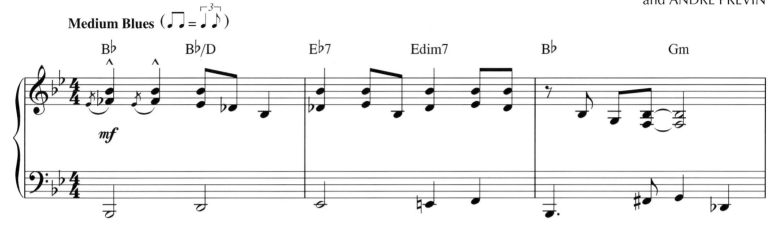

MY BABY JUST CARES FOR ME
from WHOOPEE!

Lyrics by GUS KAHN
Music by WALTER DONALDSON

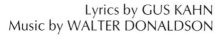

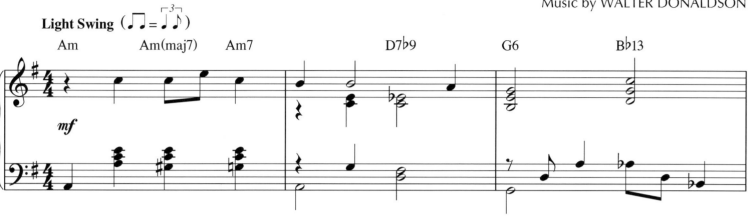

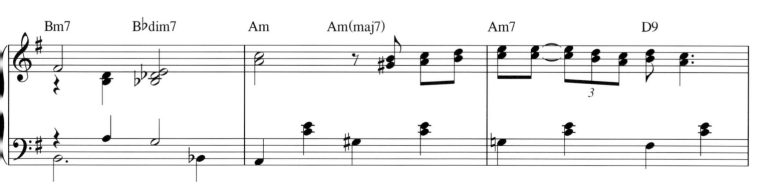

ROUTE 66

By BOBBY TROUP

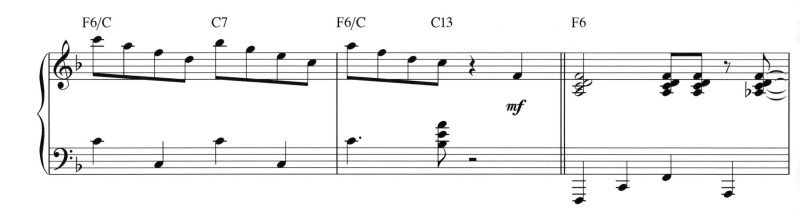

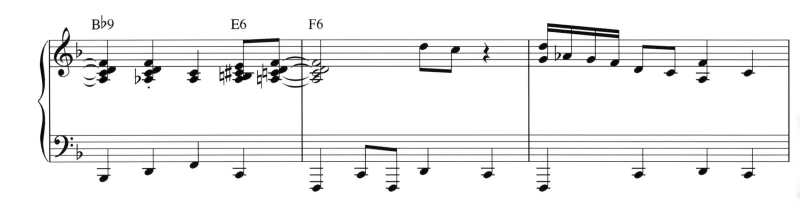

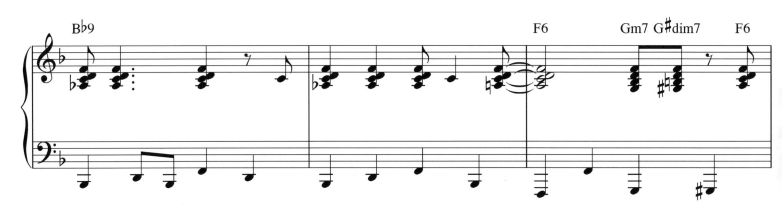

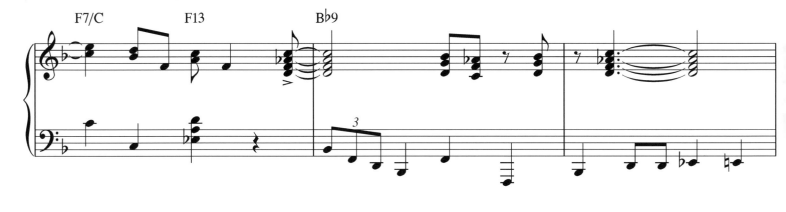

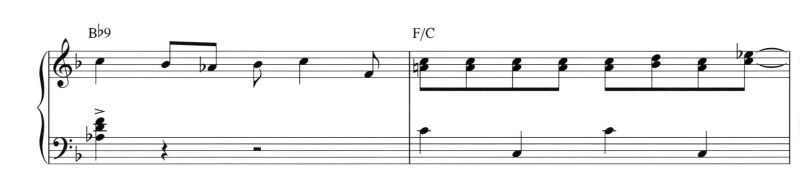

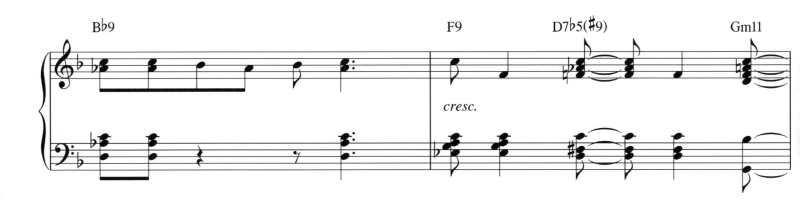

SATURDAY NIGHT
(Is the Loneliest Night of the Week)

Words by SAMMY CAHN
Music by JULE STYNE

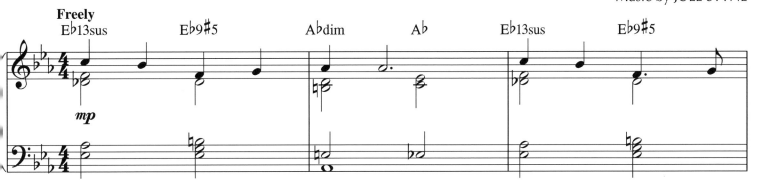

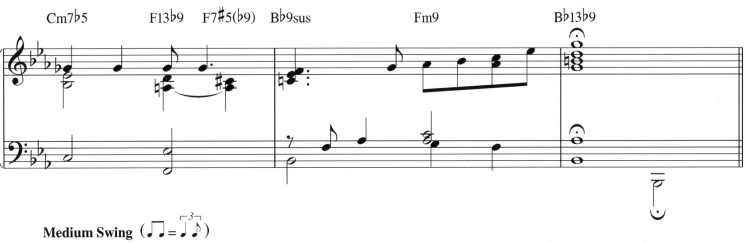

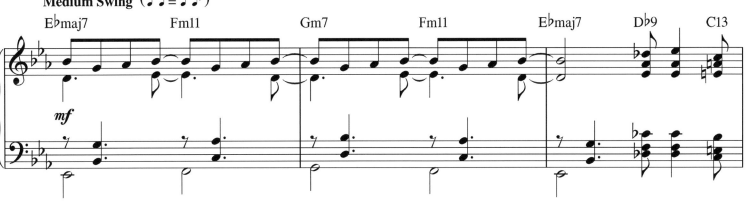

74

STEPPIN' OUT WITH MY BABY
from the Motion Picture Irving Berlin's EASTER PARADE

Words and Music by
IRVING BERLIN

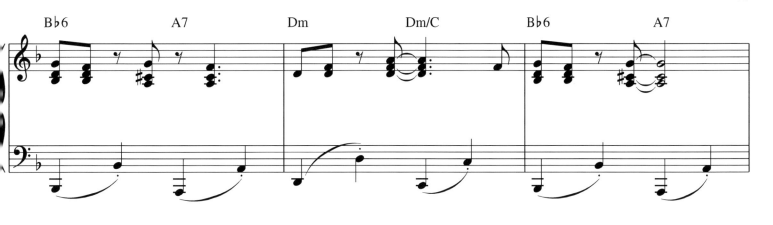

TEACH ME TONIGHT

Words by SAMMY CAHN
Music by GENE DePAUL

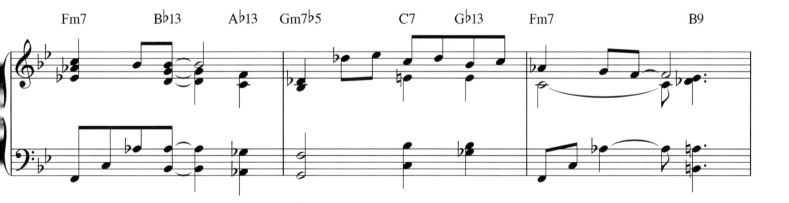

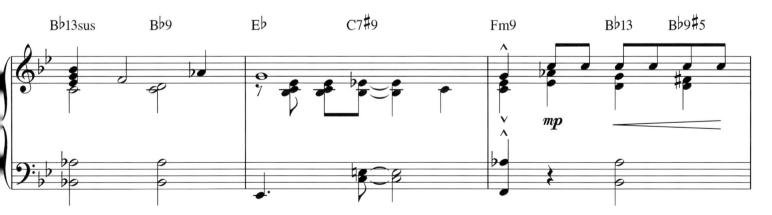

THE SWINGIN' SHEPHERD BLUES

Words and Music by MOE KOFFMAN,
RHODA ROBERTS and KENNY JACOBSON

WHEN LIGHTS ARE LOW

Words by SPENCER WILLIAMS
Music by BENNY CARTER

WITCHCRAFT

Music by CY COLEMAN
Lyrics by CAROLYN LEIGH

Bright Swing

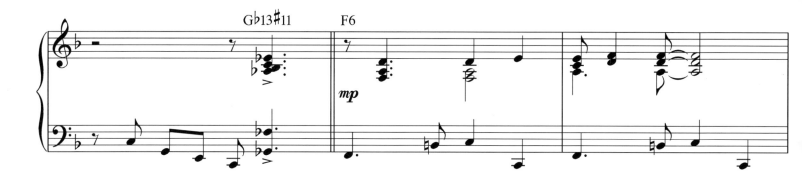

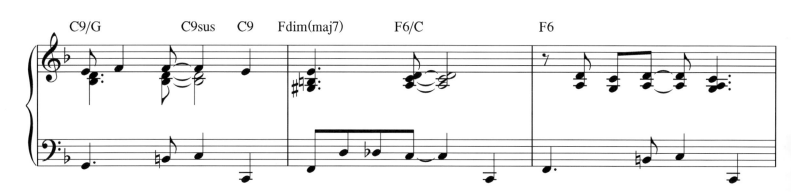